I AM JUST A TOOL IN THE HANDS OF THE CREATOR

By Sriram Nagarajan

First edition.

I am Just A Tool In The Hands Of The Creator

First Edition — 2026
ISBN: 9789358138528

Table of Contents

Preface

This book began as a question: what does it mean to be an instrument in a universe that seems at once ordered and chaotic? The opening essay—an attempt to name the feeling behind the phrase *I am just a tool in the hands of the Creator*—is not a surrender but an invitation: to look closely at agency, humility, and the strange architecture of purpose. The essay frames a larger story, and the story that follows—*A Boy Who Met God*—is both parable and report. It dramatizes an encounter that clarifies the roles played by different kinds of beings in the Creator's experiment.

The pages that follow move between reflection and narrative because the subject demands both modes. The reflective sections offer a map: terms, distinctions, and ethical implications. The narrative sections show the map in motion: how a single encounter can reveal structures of meaning that ordinary argument cannot. Read this book as both a philosophical inquiry and a witness account. If it unsettles you, let it; if it comforts you, let it. Either reaction is part of the work the book is meant to do.

My hope is modest and practical. If these pages help you hold your smallness without losing your dignity, if they invite you to act with more care while keeping your curiosity alive, then they have done their job. The Creator's experiment, as the book suggests, is not a verdict but a long conversation. This book is one voice in that conversation.

Chapter 1: I Am Just a Tool

When I say **"I am just a tool in the hands of the Creator"**, many hear resignation or helplessness. Some will think I mean I have no choice, that my life is a script written for me. Others—those bruised by loss, who watched loved ones vanish during COVID despite medicines and technologies—accept the phrase because it fits the blows they could not prevent. I do not offer an explanation; I only state the words and the images that follow.

Who am I? That question opens everything. We still do not have a proper answer about origination or about an orchestrator, if there is one. When the entire world was hit hard during COVID and near and dear ones disappeared, we saw how fragile life is. Yet despite the tragedy people moved on. Life moves on—but moving where, and why? The river flows in one direction; is there an intelligence that chooses its path? If intelligence meant linear perfection, the river's path would be straight. It is not. The river bends, finds new channels, erodes and is eroded; its nonlinear course appears as adaptation and response.

At school they gave me a book on physics. I opened it and saw pages full of text, formulas, and diagrams. How did it come all of a sudden? We know the proximate origin: minds wrote it, printers printed it, hands bound it. But the question of the origin of those minds remains. Every life on Earth carries some level of intelligence, and that intelligence decides movement. Whether to move or not is decided by one's intelligence. Sometimes I want to move on no matter what happens; sometimes movement is stopped and intelligence can do nothing but surrender and allow life to decide.

A tool in ordinary language is lifeless—a hammer, a chisel. The hammer has no intelligence; the wielder supplies skill and intent. The purpose of the hammer or chisel is to carve a stone into a sculpture. In the process the tool receives many hits, but the outcome—a stone turned into a beautiful form—is the result. The tool endures impact; the sculptor claims the form. When I say I am a tool, I place the image beside the other images I carry.

Conscious beings resist the tool metaphor because they do not want a superior to govern them. They take credit for their successes and their failures. They know what they are doing, whether good or bad, and they own the consequences. They grow, invent, and claim authorship. But can any being rely only on its intelligence forever? Suppose a conscious being wants to build something or invent something for the benefit of human beings. With intelligence and skill the being will move forward to achieve it, but what about the rest of the world around this being? Are they having the same intent to collaborate? Some may; some may not. What if the some who do not are also conscious beings? Being conscious does not mean being good; it means actions and reactions are owned and strongly believed in. Two conscious beings with different intents can both be intelligent and both be acting from conviction. How then do they collaborate when their aims diverge?

We are chasing a light at the far end of a tunnel, and we do not know where the tunnel began. We see the source of light as the destination. While we move forward chasing that light we have not seen from where we started—the beginning of the tunnel. Perhaps the tunnel is such that the source of light is both beginning and end. Time moves forward; we cannot reverse it like a video player to go back to time 00:00 and see the origin. It is not a video player that can be rewound to reveal the beginning. Time plays a role in exploration, but exploration itself happens now. Only when we reference the now to past and future does time make sense.

Imagine a glowing bulb in empty space. The glowing is the NOW; it will stop glowing in the NOW. Past and future exist in memory; the now is not memory. To be in the now is to be glowing, to be conscious without past and future. What does it mean for the now to be not glowing? Not glowing is dark, not visible, but can we say not present? To call something not present now is only possible if we know it was present before in time. That which never existed cannot be said to be not present now. Fundamentally, what we see in the now comes from a Source that exists always. If the glowing bulb stands alone in space with no objects around, it radiates light outward to the maximum it can. In the now the bulb simply radiates. If it turns off, darkness is not nothing; darkness is dormant. It is a state of the Source. The Source has the potential and the will to glow and to turn off. The Source chooses to glow to see how far its light can travel as part of an exploration to know itself.

Chapter 2: Origins and the Source

Perhaps the Creator's creation is an exploration of knowing itself, to see how far it can go. What is happening now in the world is part of that exploration. Human beings are an evolved species leading the exploration process, but we are not alone; we are supported by other sentient and no sentient things. The idea of I AM and SELF is so engrossing that we do not find the others belonging to ourselves. We feel we are a separate entity in reality and our experiences belong to ourselves. We believe our purpose is unique and individual.

Are there beings out there other than this world that are superior and more civilized than us? Maybe there are. There may be similar universes with life; we simply have not gone far enough outwardly to explore. Mystery keeps us moving. This exploration will never end if we go outwardly because technology is a limiting factor. We have taken millions of years to reach this point and may need far more time to reach other universes. Things will become interesting the day we discover life elsewhere. Are they like us, superior or inferior? Many assumptions will be challenged, and that possibility is enough to keep us moving.

When I live a conscious life I make decisions and I face the consequences because it is my intelligence. When my intelligence is with someone else and I am a tool, the decisions and their consequences are born by the owner. The tool is struck, it bears the blows, and the sculptor claims the form. Conscious beings who refuse to be tools may succeed and grow to great heights, claiming full control. But can they succeed always and rely only on their intelligence? Suppose a conscious being wants to build something for the benefit of human beings. With intelligence and skill the being will move forward to achieve it, but what about the rest of the world around this being. Are they having the same intent to collaborate? Some may and some may not. What if the some who do not are also conscious beings? Being conscious does not mean being good; it means actions and reactions are owned and strongly believed in. How does two conscious beings collaborate when their intents are different?

Sometimes alignment comes through insight, sometimes through force, sometimes through the slow work of shared purpose. Sometimes the world brings us back to a path we resisted—not to punish but to teach, to reveal a larger pattern we could not see alone. The river flows its nonlinear path for reasons we may not fully know. The physics book exists because minds wrote it, but the origin of those minds points us back to a deeper Source. The glowing bulb radiates; darkness is dormancy, not absence. The hammer and chisel are struck to create beauty; the tool bears the blows and helps reveal the form within the stone.

If we knew the Creator and the purpose of creation we would know the origin of intelligence and what makes us move. Perhaps the Creator's purpose is to know itself by exploring every possibility through its instruments. Multiple universes could be parallel laboratories of that exploration. The Source is ever-present, glowing and dormant, choosing when to radiate and when to rest. Darkness is not absence but potential. Movement is how the Creator knows itself and how we, as tools and as selves, discover what it means to be alive. The question remains: will I insist on being the maker, claiming every success and every failure as mine alone, or will I stand as an instrument that plays with skill and freedom within a larger composition?

Talking about a Creator without proof or evidence is, for many, nothing more than hallucination—a story built from longing, fear, or imagination. Stories about the Creator are plentiful; they travel in every language, in every culture. One such story is the simple, irresistible tale of "A Boy who met GOD." To the conscious mind this is a curiosity at best and a nuisance at worst: it does not fit the space of logic and evidence, so it is brushed aside. To the unconscious it is nourishment—a pattern that comforts, explains, and completes.

It is not that all conscious people deny the existence of a Creator. Many do not accept claims without evidence; they do not believe blindly. They rely on intelligence, on reason, on what can be tested and verified. Even so, consciousness is not impermeable. There are moments when intelligence is overwhelmed by circumstance—when the environment overpowers the will—and then surrender happens. In those moments, the conscious may yield and accept the

Source completely. Surrender is not always the same as belief; sometimes it is a refuge, a way to stop fighting the unanswerable.

Chapter 3: Consciousness and the World

This chapter examines how conscious and unconscious modes of being shape the world we inhabit. Consciousness brings novelty, invention, and moral imagination; it also brings ego, conflict, and the risk of stagnation when minds align too closely. Unconsciousness—understood here as a configuration that responds to a larger orchestration—provides continuity, repair, and the subtle guidance that keeps the system from collapsing under its own experiments.

Conscious beings resist the tool metaphor because they do not want a superior to govern them. They take credit for their successes and their failures. They know what they are doing, whether good or bad, and they own the consequences. They grow, invent, and claim authorship. But can any being rely only on its intelligence forever? Suppose a conscious being wants to build something or invent something for the benefit of human beings. With intelligence and skill the being will move forward to achieve it, but what about the rest of the world around this being? Are they having the same intent to collaborate?

Some may; some may not. What if the some who do not are also conscious beings? Being conscious does not mean being good; it means actions and reactions are owned and strongly believed in. Two conscious beings with different intents can both be intelligent and both be acting from conviction. How then do they collaborate when their aims diverge?

Sometimes alignment comes through insight, sometimes through force, sometimes through the slow work of shared purpose. Sometimes the world brings us back to a path we resisted—not to punish but to teach, to reveal a larger pattern we could not see alone. The river flows its nonlinear path for reasons we may not fully know. The physics book exists because minds wrote it, but the origin of those minds points us back to a deeper Source. The glowing bulb radiates; darkness is dormancy, not absence. The hammer and chisel are struck to create beauty; the tool bears the blows and helps reveal the form within the stone.

If we knew the Creator and the purpose of creation we would know the origin of intelligence and what makes us move. Perhaps the Creator's purpose is to know itself by exploring every possibility through its instruments. Multiple universes could be parallel laboratories of that exploration. The Source is ever-present, glowing and dormant, choosing when to radiate and when to rest. Darkness is not absence but potential. Movement is how the Creator knows itself and how we, as tools and as selves, discover what it means to be alive. The question remains: will I insist on being the maker, claiming every success and every failure as mine alone, or will I stand as an instrument that plays with skill and freedom within a larger composition?

Chapter 4: The Boy's Story — Arrival

The story begins on a day when every news channel carried the same breaking headline: a boy had met God and had seen God's world. At first many dismissed it as a gimmick—a manufactured sensation to boost ratings. Newsrooms, after all, are hungry for attention; audiences are scattered across platforms; anything that promises a spike in viewers is suspect. Yet the claim was simple and stubborn: a child had returned with a story no one had heard before.

People reacted in predictable ways. Sceptics said the boy must be dreaming, or mentally unstable. Believers rejoiced, each quietly certain that the boy had met their God. The boy's parents kept his photographs and details private until the interview, perhaps to protect him from a crowd, perhaps to control the narrative. Rumours multiplied as the hour approached. The story, once small, grew like a fire in dry grass.

An interview was scheduled in a large auditorium and broadcast live. A renowned anchor was given a set of questions—carefully prepared, thoughtful, designed to test and to reveal. The auditorium filled. The world tuned in. The countdown began: 9, 8, 7, 6, 5, 4, 3, 2, 1.

As the countdown ended the boy was introduced by the anchor and made comfortable to sit in the chair set for him. There was a huge cheer from the crowd which was unexpected because this boy was not known until the news channel aired about him, but somehow people cheered as if they were meeting their celebrity. The boy looked calm and composed, not perturbed by the cheering of the crowd or by seeing this big audience. He took his seat, greeting the anchor and also signed the crowd humbly as a respectful gesture. The boy's face was zoomed in by the cameras and the big screens in the auditorium were streaming it full close up. People were spellbound upon seeing the boy's face; they did not imagine the way the boy was conducting himself. He was so calm and composed, a pleasant smile on his face throughout, as if he was not affected by anything and looked like a new born baby with excitement and joy. Suddenly the cheering crowd started hushing as they could not believe what they were seeing. Just the look and conduct of the boy made their minds still. So many questions about the boy faded in everyone's mind.

They just wanted to continue to see him as he was and many felt that was enough; they all felt a kind of peace within themselves. All the rattling minds became calm and peaceful. Many felt, let this go like this forever and let the boy stay there and not speak. That was the level of intensity the boy was radiating through his presence. People started creating a respectful attitude towards the boy because they could experience a peace within upon seeing him. This is not a new experience; such experiences can be seen in newborns and children as they always show an unconditional love and we know the newborn smile is always divine. It brings a lot of joy on seeing the baby and such was the experience the boy was radiating which captivated the entire audience. The anchor was dumbstruck and it seemed the anchor had lost the intention and objective to ask the questions that were prepared for the interview. As minutes flew the crowd became pin-drop silence; it was only the natural sound that could be heard and it was a stand-still movement. The boy looked at the audience and spoke with a divine smile—**"Can we communicate verbally now?"**

Chapter 5: The Boy's Encounter

The boy's voice came like honey as he spoke, and his question—**"Can we communicate verbally now?"**—carried the quiet implication that communication had already been happening, silently, from the moment he stepped onto the dais; the connection between him and the crowd had been established in that silence, which is why many felt there was nothing more to say—the answers were already present in the stillness. The anchor, recovering his professional composure, blurted the blunt, human question: **"Are you real and can I touch you?"** The boy smiled and replied, **"I am very much real, as you are,"** and extended his hand; when the anchor shook it he felt foolish for having asked, and the boy looked into the anchor's eyes and asked, **"Hope you experienced me in physical reality?"** The closer the anchor leaned in, the more he felt drawn into a deeper space where there was nothing but peace. Still, a few in the crowd—the conscious ones, the scientists by temperament—found their intelligence interrupting the experience with the question: *How could this happen?* The anchor, bound to his script despite the moment, returned to the first question on the paper, awkwardly asking what he knew was a stupid thing to ask: "**Are you under any psychological treatment, and were you taking any medicines before you met GOD**?" The boy's reply was immediate and plain: "How does it matter? Is GOD visible only to those who are under treatment or taking such medicines? I understand what you are asking—am I hallucinating, is your question, since these psychological drugs make one hallucinate and you want to check if I am hallucinating or not?" The anchor intervened, voice small and honest: "I would not have asked such a question after seeing you and the experience you gave, but I am following my duty—this question was prepared already; in fact, I don't have any questions to ask." The boy laughed softly and said, "**I felt the same when I met GOD.**"

The boy turned to the anchor and said, "From here, let me do the talking. I am sure by the end of my speech you will have all your prepared questions answered, and the questions not on your list will be answered too. Is that fine?" The anchor nodded, smiling, and gestured, *"It's all yours."* The boy paused, drew a deep breath, scanned the auditorium, and then gently closed his eyes as if to record and absorb everything around him. With his eyes still closed he began:

I was one of you who questioned the existence of God. Thanks to my parents, who brought me into this world with an intelligence that makes me question everything, I do not accept things without asking. From the day I first spoke I asked my mother, 'Show me where God is; you praise God, but I want to see.' **She told me, 'God is everywhere; you cannot see God separately.'** I thought, how can something that is everywhere not be seen? I could find answers for most things I encountered, but not for God. I spoke to many; all they offered were references to textbooks and religious scriptures that talk about God, but none pointed to a location. In a year I read all the scriptures—they all spoke about God, but not the place where God can be seen. I was alone with my intelligence trying to tackle this question. Then one day something struck me about my mother's statement: if God is everywhere, then I should be able to know God in the things I see, including myself. **Where do I start?"**

I started by trying to understand what life is. Why do people suffer? Why am I not always happy? I have my own concerns, problems, unfulfilled desires. I noticed that those who speak most about God are often those who are unhappy with their lives, who point at God as the cause of what befalls them. The difference between them and me was simple: they pointed outward, while I accepted the problem and tried to find a solution instead of handing it off to some unseen hand.

Still, there were things I could not explain with my intelligence. I had seen people I knew in critical condition recover simply because of their faith; doctors called it a miracle. There were countless such stories, repeated enough times that I could not dismiss them all as coincidence. From that pattern I concluded that the God question could not be fully addressed by the scientific method as it stood; it required approaching a different dimension, one the scientific community had not yet mapped. Faced with that, my mind went blank. The longing to know God only intensified.

I turned inward. If God is everywhere, I told myself, then God must be discoverable in the things I see, including myself. I watched my body: organs working in harmony without my conscious direction, breath coming and going on its own. I did not look at these facts as a scientist cataloguing mechanisms; I looked at them as a child seeing a masterpiece. I bowed, not in ritual but in recognition—what I saw around me was not something I had made. My intelligence softened into humility. The arrogance that once felt like knowledge shrank to a seed beside the vastness of what I observed.

Humility did not become blind faith. I kept my questions and my reasoning, but my posture toward the world changed. My agitation to prove or disprove God eased; I simply wanted to know. Conviction about the possibility of a Creator grew, but I guarded my ego so that certainty would not become pride. I began a practice: whenever I had a moment, I would dissolve into silence, simply to be calm and to watch what happened inside me. All my questions kept returning to one: **Who am I?** If I could answer that, perhaps the rest would fall into place.

I lived with that seed of inquiry, patient and without a timetable. My mother had always told me to pray before sleep, and I had done it for her sake. One night, lying down,

I closed my eyes and prayed in a way I never had before: *My mother believes you exist and says you are everywhere. If you are real, show me. I am not good enough to see you on my own. I have nothing else to ask; seeing you would be enough for my whole life.* For the first time, I slept with an empty mind.

Chapter 6: The Revelation

I remember clearly: someone woke me from sleep. I opened my eyes to a bright light around me and my mind, at once alert, asked what this unusual thing could be. Then a voice spoke again, urging me to step into the light. I wondered why there should be any drama—why not come plainly? The voice answered that all my questions would be answered, but I had to take the next step: step into the bright light. Humility rose in me, and I stepped forward. What followed felt like being carried through a tunnel; I was transported and then landed in a place that looked, at first glance, like a vast manufacturing plant.

People moved about the place, and to my astonishment every face was familiar. I knew, with a certainty that was not dreamlike, that I was not imagining this, though my eyes struggled to accept it. I kept myself humble and simply observed. A hand touched my shoulder; I turned and saw a pleasant, familiar face asking, **"Shall we go?"** I answered yes and, almost reflexively, asked, **"Are you real? Can I touch you?"** The reply was gentle: **"I am very much real,**

as you are." With both hands on my shoulders they said, **"Let's go,"** and I followed.

We entered the vast workshop. Rows of lab-like stations unfolded before me; prototypes and models of everything I knew in the world were arranged there. Before I could ask, they said, **"This is where creation is designed. All that you see in your world is designed here. We are part of the Creator's design house. From amoeba to human, everything is created here. If you wish, you may see them all."** I remembered what I had asked earlier and said again, **"Can I see the GOD?"** They smiled and replied, **"Of course—follow me."** As we moved through the setup I could see all that exists in the world as prototypes here. I asked why the faces I recognized were present here, though those people lived in the world. They answered, **"It is maya; what you see here is your own reflection. In truth, those you see here have no fixed identity. They do not appear here as they do in your world, but we tuned your perception so you would recognize them with familiar faces."** Hearing this, I felt the technology of my world shrink in comparison, and my humility before creation deepened as we moved toward the place where I would meet God.

They warned me that the meeting and what I would see might vanish from my memory if I revealed it in the world I lived in. I accepted the condition and stepped forward. I entered the room of GOD—the long-awaited moment of my life.

For the first time I saw God, and the face was familiar—yet I had already understood that it was Maya, so how God looked no longer mattered to me. I thought, what is there to ask? A reply came into my mind: Go ahead. I realized then that our communication was not spoken aloud but telepathic.

I asked, Why all this? What is the purpose? What is your plan? How did you first come? Who created you? What is the origin of everything? Why do people suffer and why is there disparity?

God answered: **I AM everywhere; there is no place where I am not, and there is nothing apart from Me. All that is, is Me—including you. You are my creation**

and are made out of Me, not separate. I am present always and real.

I replied, You are repeating what the scriptures say; that does not show me evidence. I need evidence of what you say—I want to see.

God: That is true; the scriptures say what I am telling you now. The evidence is before you—you are speaking to it through your mind. Is that not enough? Your doubts arise from the limits of your body and mind; you cannot perceive as I perceive. If you could perceive as I do, you would have no questions. You are created out of Me but with limits so you can explore away from Me; I am complete and have nothing to gain or lose. Maya is the built-in mechanism that keeps you away from Me so you can explore the world with your body-mind limits.

I asked, Why all this? In this body-mind limit people suffer—do you not see? Your exploration is at the cost of beings who think they are separate from you and who suffer.

God: You know the answer yourself. Suffering is not ultimately real; the moment individual identity is foregone, one will see oneself as Me and will simply play the role assigned.

I asked, Why do some believe in you and some do not? Why do you help some and not others? Why this inequality?

God: All beings were created with intelligence to conduct themselves consciously. If all beings acted the same, evolution would stall—like robots on an assembly line. Difference and inequality drive evolution; different minds and conditions push life to adapt. What you see here is feedback from your world used to redesign everything. I am part of the exploration, making it better and better. One day this exploration will end and begin anew; there are multiple worlds exploring in parallel, different from yours. If you ask when it all started or when it will end: to start, something must be present—and that which is present always has no beginning. Other than Me, everything is Maya; in Maya everything happens and it conceals Me, and only a few see through the Maya.

I asked, Who are those who see you through Maya? Are there beings you take care of in the Maya world?

God: Yes. There are two kinds of beings: the conscious and the unconscious. Conscious beings arose when the world first gained awareness; they make choices, good or bad, and sometimes believe themselves to be gods separate from Me. These conscious beings have strong ego and identity; they attribute success to themselves. Their approach can harm other conscious beings. Thus the creation of the unconscious became necessary. The unconscious are My tools, governed by Me. Conscious beings do not need Me directly because their body-mind configuration resists external input. While conscious beings drive the world, the unconscious support them through Me.

Who are the unconscious? They are those in whom belief in Me is ingrained in their body-mind configuration, though they appear ordinary to the world. They live on their own and possess intelligence like conscious beings, but they use it when I ask them to, to support a general cause driven by conscious beings. They are messengers who do not compete with conscious beings; if they try, they fail, and in time they learn they are unconscious—tools in the hands of God. Whether conscious or unconscious, all belong to Me; it is a play to explore possibilities.

Listening, I was spellbound; everything became clear. The one thing I had been searching for—the source that sent me to explore—was before me. I asked, I was told that all that happened here will vanish from my memory if I reveal it to the world. Why is that so?

God: It would hinder the evolution and exploration. If beings knew the truth behind Maya, would they still evolve? I ask you now: after knowing this truth, do you have any intent to live your life and explore?

I said, I am content with what I am; there is nothing out there to explore—it is all Maya. Then I asked what I should do when I return to the world.

God replied, You should develop the art of acting seriously after knowing the truth—which is simply to play the role you are assigned.

Chapter 7: Aftermath

I opened my eyes gently and found the audience and the anchor beside me. I asked the anchor, **"Is there any question about God?"** A hand rose from the crowd; the anchor passed the mic to the man. Everyone watched him closely, curious whether anything more could be asked after my speech had seemed to answer so much. The gentleman leaned forward and asked, **"The God you met— which religion He belongs to?"** I felt a cold certainty that this was Maya at work: the body-mind configuration of the world folding even God into familiar categories. The man pressed on, earnest and insistent—he said he believed me and wanted confirmation that the God I had seen was the God of his religion. The fragile peace in the auditorium shattered. Voices rose, accusations and shouts replaced silence, and the question became a spark for conflict: *your God, my God.* Conscious sceptics and atheists shouted that this proved nothing; believers argued that it proved everything. The atmosphere turned volatile. My parents, standing behind the stage, grew anxious as the crowd began to surge; I could see groups moving as if to seize an answer by force. The anchor tried to calm people, but no one would listen. Realizing the danger, he called my parents to the stage and signalled police to escort me out. In a scramble I was led away by a different route so the crowd could not see me. Authorities advised that we leave the city for a while; we were taken to an airport and flown by private jet to an unknown place. My father, worried but grateful, spoke with officials and thanked the government for rescuing their son. As I sat by the jet window watching the world shrink below, I replayed the moment and realized I should have anticipated such a question and prepared an answer—any answer would be folded back into someone's faith; it was a trap. Then a thought struck me and I smiled; my mother, sitting beside me, asked what was wrong. I looked at her and simply smiled, because the gentleman who had raised the question was one of the familiar faces I had seen in the God-world—an unconscious being, a tool in the hands of God, placed to ask exactly that question so the exploration could continue.

Chapter 8: Conscious and Unconscious Beings

The Creator's experiment, as I understood it in that room, is not a simple binary of free will versus fate. It is a vast, layered theatre in which different kinds of players perform complementary roles. To speak plainly: there are **conscious beings** and **unconscious beings**, and both are necessary for the exploration the Creator has set in motion. Understanding their functions clarifies why the world appears as it does—full of conflict, invention, suffering, and sudden grace.

The conscious being — agency, conviction, and the engine of change

Conscious beings are the agents of novelty. They are the minds that reflect, plan, invent, and insist. They claim authorship of their actions and accept the consequences. Their intelligence is active and self-referential: they ask *why*, they design, they resist, and they assert identity. This is the species that builds civilizations, debates ethics, and pushes technology forward.

- **Strengths:** creativity, initiative, moral imagination, capacity for large-scale coordination.
- **Weaknesses:** ego, rigidity, the tendency to mistake local success for universal truth; when many conscious beings align in the same conviction, evolution can stall because diversity of intent is reduced.

Consciousness drives the world because it generates difference. Where all minds think alike, there is no pressure to adapt; where minds differ, new solutions and new forms emerge. In that sense, conscious beings are the engine of evolution—often messy, sometimes cruel, but indispensable for novelty.

The unconscious being — the tool, the support, the hidden hand

Unconscious beings are not lesser; they are different in design and function. They are the instruments through which the Creator subtly guides outcomes without overriding the autonomy of conscious agents. Their body-mind configuration is tuned to respond to the Creator's input; belief in the Source is woven into their being. To the world they appear ordinary, but their role is to support, to nudge, to sustain patterns that conscious beings alone cannot maintain.

- **Function:** act as stabilizers, messengers, and facilitators of larger designs; they enable feedback loops between the Creator's intent and the unfolding world.
- **Behavior:** they do not compete with conscious beings; when they attempt to, they fail and learn their place as instruments.
- **Moral posture:** they are not puppets in a moral sense; they exercise intelligence, but their intelligence is aligned with a broader orchestration.

Unconscious beings make possible the continuity of exploration. They are the quiet hands that hold the scaffolding while conscious beings build and demolish, learn and err.

Why both are necessary for evolution

Evolution, in the Creator's design, requires **difference** and **support** simultaneously. Conscious beings introduce difference—new aims, conflicting values, experiments in living. Without them, the system becomes inert. Unconscious beings provide the **contextual stability** that allows experiments to be meaningful rather than catastrophic. They are the buffers, the repair mechanisms, the invisible infrastructure that keeps the game playable.

Think of it as an ecosystem: predators and prey, pollinators and plants. Each role exists not because it is morally superior but because it contributes to the system's capacity to explore possibilities. The Creator's aim—to know itself through multiplicity—needs both the boldness of conscious agents and the fidelity of unconscious instruments.

The ethics of being a tool and the responsibility of consciousness

If some of us are tools by design, what does that mean for moral responsibility? Two practical truths emerge:

1. **Conscious beings bear responsibility for the consequences of their choices.** Claiming agency means accepting the moral weight of outcomes.

Evolution advances when conscious agents act with awareness of the wider web they affect.

2. **Unconscious beings embody a different responsibility: fidelity to purpose without domination.** Their moral task is not to dominate but to support the flourishing of the whole. When they act, they do so as part of a larger choreography.

For those who discover they are "tools"—whether by inclination, temperament, or revelation—the ethical path is humility and skill. Humility recognizes that one is part of a larger composition; skill honours the craft of playing one's role well. For conscious agents, the ethical path is to cultivate discernment: to know when to insist, when to yield, and how to design systems that minimize needless suffering.

Practical implications for living and for evolution

- **Cultivate humility without surrendering agency.** Humility reduces destructive ego; agency preserves the capacity to innovate. Both are needed.

- **Design institutions that respect difference.** Systems that punish divergence or enforce uniformity will stagnate; systems that channel difference into constructive feedback will accelerate evolution.
- **Value the unseen supports.** Unconscious roles—caregivers, quiet organizers, those who sustain culture—are not second-class; they are essential. Recognizing and honouring them stabilizes societies.
- **Act as if you are both tool and author.** In practice, this means doing your work with excellence while remembering you are part of a larger story.

A final note on meaning and the Creator's orchestration

If the Creator's purpose is to know itself by exploring every possibility, then the world's contradictions—cruelty and kindness, genius and error, suffering and healing—are not failures but data. Conscious beings generate the data;

unconscious beings preserve the conditions for learning. Together they make the Creator's self-inquiry possible.

To live with this understanding is not to resign oneself to passivity. It is to accept a paradox: **we are instruments and authors at once.** We can play our assigned roles with devotion and, within those roles, exercise creativity and compassion. That is the art the Creator invites us to learn—to act seriously, to play fully, and to hold both our smallness and our significance with equal grace.

Epilogue

The boy's story ends not with a final answer but with an invitation: to live differently in light of what one has seen. Knowing that some of us are instruments does not strip life of meaning; it reframes meaning. If the Creator's experiment is to know itself through multiplicity, then every small act—every kindness, every invention, and every failure—becomes a note in a vast composition.

If you carry this book's central image—the tool and the sculptor—into your days, let it change how you act. When you succeed, remember the hands that steadied the scaffold. When you fail, remember the larger pattern that may yet be revealed. When you meet another person, consider whether they are playing a conscious role or an unconscious one, and treat both with respect.

The final lesson is practical and humane: **play your role with excellence and humility.** Do your work well. Love the people around you. Keep asking the hard questions, but let some of them rest while you act. In the end, the Creator's experiment is not a test to pass or fail; it is a long, patient process of discovery. To be a tool is not to be diminished; it is to be entrusted. Take that trust seriously, and you will have lived well.